Successful
Mentoring
in a week

*Stephen Carter
and Gareth Lewis*

ton

British Library Cataloguing in Publication Data

Lewis, Gareth
Successful Mentoring in a Week
I. Title II. Carter, Stephen
658.3124

ISBN 0 340 61137 5

First published 1994
Impression number   10   9   8   7   6   5   4   3   2   1
Year   1999   1998   1997   1996   1995   1994

Typeset by Multiplex Techniques Ltd, St Mary Cray, Kent.
Printed for Hodder & Stoughton Educational, a division of
Hodder Headline Plc, 338 Euston Road, London NW1 3BH by
Colorcraft Ltd, Hong Kong

ⓘⓜ the Institute of Management

F O U N D A T I O N

The Institute of Management (IM) is at the forefront of management development and best management practice. The Institute embraces all levels of management from students to chief executives. It provides a unique portfolio of services for all managers, enabling them to develop skills and achieve management excellence.

For information on the benefits of membership, please contact:

Department HS
Institute of Management
Cottingham Road
Corby
Northants NN17 1TT

Tel. 0536 204222
Fax 0536 201651

This series is commissioned by the Institute of Management Foundation.

C O N T E N T S

■ I N T R O D U C T I O N ■

Many organisations are already benefiting from in-company mentoring programmes and schemes. Other organisations are looking for ways to make management development programmes more effective.

Successful Mentoring in a Week is written for those who wish to know more about the subject and its benefits, as well as those who are involved in mentoring, or managing a mentoring programme.

The approach to the subject outlined in this book was gained principally from the experience of the authors in the development of the highly successful Institute of Management Competent Manager Programme, which is a mentor-supported distance learning programme leading to a nationally approved qualification in management. However, the book tackles the subject in a general way which is appropriate to many different development contexts. Many of these are covered in the Friday section.

The book provides a step-by-step guide through the process and we will cover:

Sunday	What is mentoring?
Monday	What makes a successful mentor?
Tuesday	The four bases of mentoring
Wednesday	The development base
Thursday	The interpersonal base
Friday	The context base
Saturday	Implementing mentoring programmes

What is mentoring?

Before we go on to look at the skills and the practice of mentoring, we should give some thought to the concept of mentoring, and what it is. Today we will look at:

- What mentoring is
- The benefits of mentoring
- The process of mentoring

In recent years, the idea of mentoring has appeared in the management development lexicon. You could therefore be forgiven for thinking that it was a new idea. However, like most good ideas, it has been around for a long time. In fact, the term comes from Greek mythology when Ulysses left his son, Telemachus under the tutelage of his old friend Mentor.

In the modern era, you might frequently come across the term in many areas of human activity, from sports through to the arts, as well as in management.

Think about these examples:

- The old boxer who takes a young boxer under his wing, trains him and advises him while his career progresses
- The manager who recruits a new employee, and spends time with them showing them the ropes about the organisation and the job
- The manager who has been trained to support and advise an employee on an Institute of Management Certificate programme
- The team leader of a typing pool to whom all the others go when they have problems

These examples differ in terms of how systematic they are, and in their levels of formality. However, they are all examples of mentoring in action.

If you think about your personal experience at work, you will probably also realise that you have either had a mentor (or more than one), or have been a mentor. This is important because it tells us two things. First, most of us already know a lot about mentoring (even if we didn't know the term). Second, it illustrates that mentoring is an effective and natural component of good management.

So what is mentoring in a development context? We can describe it as:

a process where one person offers help, guidance, advice and support to facilitate the learning or development of another person.

It usually involves some of the following characteristics:

- The mentor is older
- The mentor is more experienced
- The mentor is more senior
- The mentor has knowledge and skills to pass on

It is worth emphasising that mentoring is not an additional management task. Its main function is to enhance performance and to support people in their natural development.

It is clear from these examples that a great deal of mentoring has gone on over the years, although it may not always have been called mentoring, and may not even have been recognised as such.

Similarly, we would contend that good managers have always been good mentors. What has changed more recently is that management commentators and educators have recognised the benefits and have tried to approach and use the concept more systematically. So much so that mentoring is now used in a planned way in many contexts. Some examples include:

- Induction training
- Career progression
- Managing projects
- Mutual mentoring in change situations
- Formal learning programmes

The benefits of mentoring

This passing on of knowledge and understanding, 'showing people the ropes', has many benefits. These benefits can be gained if the mentoring happens as a natural and informal aspect of the management process, or if it is part of a more structured and systematic development programme. We can look at these potential benefits from three points of view:

- The mentee (we shall call them learners)
- The mentor
- The organisation

Clearly, the learner has much to gain from such a relationship, although exactly what they gain will depend on the skill of the mentor and the nature of the programme.

Benefits to the learner

- Getting to know the culture and political ropes of an organisation
- Developing skills
- Receiving feedback on performance
- Access to resources
- Increased clarity and definition of goals

It would be easy to think of mentoring as a 'give' relationship, but our experience has shown that the process also offers benefits to the mentor.

Benefits to the mentor

- Assists in management tasks such as monitoring performance, communication, etc.
- Increases satisfaction and reward in the job
- Increases motivation and performance of mentored staff
- Assists personal self-development

Anything that enhances good relationships among staff is bound to have benefit for the organisation involved. However, there are some further, specific benefits for organisations in structured mentoring programmes.

Benefits for the organisation

- Improved succession planning
- More effective management development
- Faster induction of new employees
- Improved communications
- Reduced training costs
- Reduced turnover
- Increased productivity

The process of mentoring

Clearly, many of these benefits can result from both formal and informal mentoring. However, we intend in this book to concentrate on planned and systematic programmes.

Mentoring programmes, or programmes with a mentoring component are very much like any other management process.

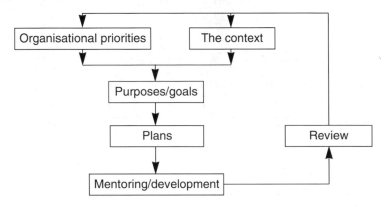

This external loop looks at the whole process from the point of view of the organisation.

Purposes or goals
As with any other project, the purposes of the programme need to be defined. Not only do they need to be stated, but they need to be agreed and communicated.

Within the totality of the programme (which will relate to the goals of the organisation), there needs to be a statement of the purpose of the mentoring component of the programme. If there is a lack of clarity here, there is a possibility of conflict between the mentoring relationship (the needs of the individual) and the greater goals of the project (the needs of the organisation). This will be dealt with in more detail in further sections.

Plans

Again, the outcomes and achievements from the programme need specifying and relating to a time frame. The principles are the same as those for any other project.

Resourcing

Resourcing in this context refers specifically to the selection and training of the mentors. This training needs to cover both the nature of the programme itself and the skills of mentoring.

Mentoring

This is the internal loop that defines the nature of the mentoring relationship itself.

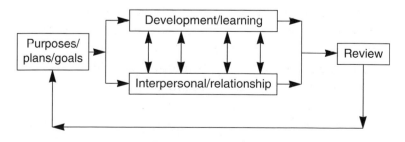

The process has two major aspects:

- Developmental/learning
- Interpersonal/relationship

These form two of the four bases of mentoring that are covered later in the week.

Summary

Today, we have looked at mentoring as a whole and seen that it brings many benefits to both the learner and the mentor. We've also seen that it can be used in various situations to aid development. The process though remains basically the same and involves purposes, plans and resources.

Tomorrow we will go on to look at what makes a successful mentor.

What makes a successful mentor?

Having looked at some of the things that mentors might do for an individual or an organisation, we now need to look at how mentors might achieve these things. And further, we need to start to consider what skills and qualities a mentor needs to be successful in this role.

- Expectations of learners
- What mentors do
- Who can be a mentor?
- Role models

Expectations of learners

A useful way of describing the sorts of things a mentor needs to do to help a learner is to look at the situation through the eyes of the learner. What does the learner need?

A mentor is supporting the development of an individual and will need to consider the:

- Particular motivation and goals of the learner
- Commitment and resources of his or her organisation to help an individual meet those goals
- Skills of the learner

A key criteria for successful mentoring must be the ability of a mentor to respond to these three factors in a positive and useful way.

A mentor therefore, needs to be able to understand what is motivating an individual to learn in the first place. Of course, there are many different factors in the motivation to learn and mentors should try and understand the particular goals of whoever they are trying to mentor. There are however, some commonalities. These might include:

- Problems to deal with
- Career progression
- Increased job satisfaction
- Personal development
- Increased performance
- Achieving organisation goals

The last of these common goals raises an interesting point. Who is setting the learner's goals? If they are set by the organisation, then a mentor needs very quickly to understand what an individual's motivation is towards

achieving these goals. One hundred per cent commitment is an easy but often erroneous assumption to make.

Successful mentoring needs resourcing. Resources include time, materials, and work, and mentors can take a vital role in securing these, particularly when an organisation has not adequately thought through its responsibilities in developing staff.

A mentor needs to be able to support a learner in regard to the particular strengths and weaknesses a learner has in the process of development. Whatever the specific functional or technical skills, a learner will probably need to employ some of the following:

- Learning skills
- Setting goals
- Identifying own learning needs
- Planning their own learning
- Listening
- Accepting help and feedback
- Taking risks

So what do mentors do?

We said that mentors facilitate and support the learning and development of others. But how do they do this?

This will differ from person to person and will depend, to some extent, on the purpose and nature of the context in which it takes place.

However, the following list is a good description of the general tasks involved in the process arising from the learner needs outlined above.

- Provide resources and opportunities for development
- Help learners to set high but achievable goals, and make realistic plans
- Monitor progress and provide feedback
- Provide a role model and pass on skills
- Assist the learner in solving problems
- Provide personal support and motivation

In undertaking these tasks, successful mentors will be doing so in a way that does not just 'go through the motions'. Nearly all learners, whatever development they are undertaking, will at some time find it daunting and possibly stressful. As important as the technical expertise and knowledge that they bring to a mentoring relationship, mentors therefore also need to provide social and emotional support. Often it is this aspect of a mentor's behaviour that will determine the success or otherwise of the mentoring relationship.

Who can be a mentor?

This is quite an ambitious list and you might wonder who these paragons of virtue are that are able to perform all of these tasks. One answer to that question is to think again of your own personal experience, and of those people who have helped and supported you at some time in your professional life. It is likely that you will soon be able to define a positive role model. It is also possible that you may think of a few negative role models that show you exactly how not to do it!

But it is true that good mentors do have certain skills and qualities that predispose them to be good mentors. Later in the week we will propose a model of the whole process that will enable us to define the skills required. Today, we want to suggest a set of qualities that you should look for in selecting mentors, or seek to develop in yourself.

Mentor qualities

Undoubtedly one of the key qualities a mentor must have is *relevant work experience*. It is not that mentors need to be a theoretical expert in a particular field, nor as we shall see, is their role centrally one of being a tutor. But mentors will need an understanding, which may be partly intuitive, of what a learner is trying to achieve. Related to this is that mentors also ideally need *experience* or *knowledge of the organisation* in which the mentoring relationship takes place. Furthermore, they need to understand through this experience 'how things get done around here' and be able to mobilise organisational support and opportunities to help a learner's development. Mentors, of course, need excellent *interpersonal skills*. They need to be good at asking questions, they need to be good listeners, they need to appear supportive and flexible in their approach and need to come across as people genuinely interested in the development of others. Finally mentors should be *good role models*. They should be credible to a learner, demonstrating an open approach, accessibility and many of the key behaviours that a learner might be trying to develop (such as personal organisation, management style etc.).

The list above can be used for the purposes of self-assessment. Use the blank form to rate yourself (or get others to rate you) on a 1 to 5 rising scale against each of the qualities. This might give you some ideas about your own development needs as a potential mentor.

	1	2	3	4	5
Work experience					
Organisation experience					
Relevant interpersonal skills					
Role model					

You should keep these in mind as you read through the rest of this book, which will discuss these issues in much more detail, hopefully giving you the information you need to develop yourself as a mentor.

Role models

Perhaps one of the best ways to discover how to mentor is to consider the people who have helped you learn and develop through your career. Consider for a moment what it was about them that was particularly useful. What made the difference for you? What did they do well, what was it they said, did, arranged that was important to you in your career development? Without over-analysing their attitudes and behaviour, a very good way of starting to enhance your skills as a mentor is simply to copy their approach. The insights and understanding will come later as you experience the role of helping others develop for yourself.

Alternatively you could consider someone whose career has flourished despite their inattention to the ideas of good practice that we have set out. Thinking of their attitudes and behaviour will give you help in understanding what might be expected of a mentor, by doing the opposite to them.

Do any of these fairy godmothers and wicked uncles ring any bells?

Fairy godmothers
'Managementors' do two things well. First, they have the personal skills to manage the process itself. This involves time management and the ability to plan, set goals and action plans, and deliver objectives.

Second, they have knowledge, skills and experience of the substantive areas of learning.

'Agreementors' have the ability to give responsibility at the right time and in the right way. They have the skills to delegate and negotiate to a high degree. They are therefore, also *'empowermentors'* with a flair for appropriately releasing responsibility.

The *'developmentor'* believes in the development of him/herself and of others. He/she intuitively seems to know what people need to understand and learn and this is demonstrated by their words and deeds. Developmentors will have a track record of involvement in the learning and development of themselves and others.

'Experimentors' are tolerant of ambiguity, are happy to try things out for themselves and encourage others to do the same. They often question the status quo and never assume that they – or anyone else – has all the answers. They understand that learning is about making mistakes and can accept failure if it results from the right motives and intent.

The *'implementor'* gets things done. They can transform thoughts and ideas into action. They know where to find the resources required, and the information and support that will make the difference. Implementors tend to be pragmatic, action oriented, and are usually good problem-solvers.

They are often close relatives of the *'achievementor'*, who sets and delivers high but achievable goals, and expects others to do the same.

'Assessmentors' can provide feedback that is clear, open and unbiased. They are critical in an objective way, i.e. not afraid to report what they see whether it is positive or negative. They do this in a way that avoids blame, personal comments, judgements but, instead, focuses on the future. Their honesty is accepted because they build up trust, demonstrating interest and care for others and offering any comments with appropriate timing.

Wicked uncles
'Argumentors' involve themselves at a subjective level. They can appear to be 'interviewing' in conversation, seeking to influence, interpret and ascribe hidden motives. They are unable to tolerate different points of view and seek to bring others, through challenge, around to their point of view. Closely related to the *'judgementor'* who is inflexible, critical, and always right. They should try agreeing and listening (see agreementor).

Far too directive, *'regimentors'* never let people try things out for themselves or do things in a different way. They only ever see one way of doing things – their way! They have a strong tendency to impose goals, timetables, solutions and opinions. They should try flexibility and empowering behaviour (see developmentor and empowermentor).

'Cementors' have a tendency to get people stuck – and leave them to dry! They hate change and regard organisational structures as something designed to fix people into roles.

Changing roles and responsibilities upsets them. They firmly believe that people should know their place. Often heard to say – when confronted with a new idea – that they've seen it all before. They should try commitment, flexibility, problem-solving (see managementor, experimentor).

The biggest failing for *'commentors'* is that they talk too much. They have an opinion on everything. They also have a tendency to think that they are right, and can easily drop into playing the expert. What they are not good at is listening. They should try listening and giving responsibility (see agreementor, developmentor).

Summary

To be a successful mentor then, we need to possess certain qualities and skills which will help us meet the expectations of the mentoring role. We need to be able to set suitable tasks and monitor the learner's progress, providing help and encouragement along the way; as well as problem-solving and providing resources. We need to aim to be a 'Fairy Godmother' and not a 'Wicked Uncle'! Tomorrow we will go on to discover the four bases of mentoring.

The four bases of mentoring

Today we will look at:

- The four bases of mentoring
- The organisational base
- Organisational readiness
- Positional strength

Having set the background we can now go on to look in more detail at the tasks and processes involved in mentoring.

We will do this by proposing a model that describes the four dimensions or bases of competence involved in mentoring. They describe a sequence and areas of activity, as well as a means for measuring strengths and weaknesses of mentors, schemes, and participating organisations.

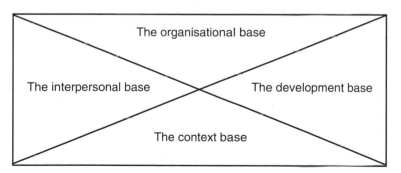

These bases are shown in the diagram, and we will analyse each one in turn over the next four days, beginning today with the organisational base. Before we do that, we should give a brief description of each.

The organisational base

This base relates to the positional strength of the individual mentor (or team of mentors) within the organisation, and to the readiness or 'fit' of the process to the culture of the organisation. Mentoring is much less likely to succeed if it does not have legitimacy and support from the organisation as a whole, and particularly from senior management. The positional strength of mentors shows commitment, but also puts into the system a substantial core of expertise, experience and knowledge of the organisation.

It is related to the qualities of management perspective, organisational know-how and credibility.

Interpersonal or relationship base

Any structured relationship requires commitment and skills to understand and empathise with the needs of others. In many ways, this is the core area of skill, because without it the rest will not follow.

It is related to the qualities of accessibility and communication.

The developmental or learning base

Most contexts in which mentoring is featured have learning or development as a component. It is therefore important that mentors have some understanding about the notion of learning, particularly about learning at work.

This base is related to the qualities of developmental orientation and flexibility.

The context base

This base involves the purposes of the developmental relationship. The requirements will change depending on whether the context is formal or informal, whether it is a structured programme of learning, and so on. It also has a limiting or defining effect on the other three bases.

We will now go on to study each of these bases in more detail.

The organisational base

The organisational base of mentoring has two major dimensions. These are:

- Organisational readiness
- Positional strength

In this base, we focus on the need for the process in the organisation, on the culture and power structures within which it will take place, and on the ability of the mentors to implement or deliver the scheme.

In fact, the second and third facets are very closely related, but are set out first from the perspective of the organisation as a whole, then from that of the individual mentors.

Organisational readiness

We can describe the differences between organisations in a number of ways. Even organisations which are involved in the same business can go about it in quite different ways. Those differences can be described in a number of ways. The kinds of distinctions that are often used include:

- Different structures and methods of organisation
- Different styles of management
- Different cultures
- Different systems
- Different ways of making decisions – both formal and informal

Consider these two theoretical examples:

A civil service department. It is hierarchical and bureaucratic. People in positions of authority are usually there for their professional or technical expertise rather than management competence. People are expected to do what they are told. Mistakes are framed as failure, and are not tolerated. There is a correct way to do everything, and innovation is not sought. Change is considered as a threat.

A young software company. This company is quite small (80 employees) and has an atmosphere more like a club. There is no rigid or hierarchical management structure as the staff work in teams. It works on a project-by-project basis in teams, and the opinions and contributions of all staff are invited and valued. It lives and works in a fast-paced and innovative environment. Cooperation is seen as the key to the company's success.

The question that we shall be interested in is whether these two different companies can both support successful mentoring schemes. The answer, of course, is that it is possible. However, experience tells us that one of them is much more likely to be suited to support the learning and development of its staff at work.

An individual informal mentoring relationship can thrive and be successful in almost any environment, but is easier and more likely to succeed in the right environment. Systematic mentoring schemes can only succeed where the right conditions prevail.

It is not a simple matter of saying that mentoring will not work with certain styles of management, although it is precisely these kinds of influences that affect the success of mentoring within an organisation.

Some of the factors that are known to be conducive to the notion of mentoring are included in the checklist below:

- A supportive culture
- Unintentional failure is tolerated
- Job roles are flexible
- Staff are respected and consulted

- Staff are given authority to make decisions
- Open communication is encouraged
- There is high concern for people

It is worth giving due consideration to these factors when thinking about the appropriateness of a potential mentoring scheme within an organisation. Realistically though, there are many organisations who do not correspond to the above profile in every detail. Equally, there are organisations where mentoring is seen as a part of the way to changing.

In these cases mentoring can succeed, but two further elements need to be strongly in place.

Visible top management support

This is necessary for two reasons. First, it is a declaration of intention and importance. Top management support communicates a powerful message about the need for change, and the ways it can be achieved.

Second, a scheme supported by the senior management is likely to receive the practical resourcing necessary to make such a scheme a success.

Developmental bias
There needs to be a shared understanding that only by developing people can an organisation change and improve performance. Added to this, there needs to be an appreciation that real learning can take place at work, as well as in the classroom or training room.

In other words, there needs to be shared recognition, not **that** learning is important, but **how** it can happen.

For this reason the success of many schemes can be attributed to the efforts of a 'champion' who can communicate with and persuade, senior management about the benefits of the style of learning implicit in many mentoring schemes.

Positional strength

This leads us on to consideration of the position of the individual mentor within the organisation. This positional strength of the mentor is important because of the credibility of the scheme, which will effect its chances of success.

It is also important because positional strength will influence access to available resources. Mentoring efforts can founder for lack of resources – particularly time and training.

The following checklist provides a set of indicators about the optimum conditions for successful mentoring.

	1	2	3	4	5
Positional strength					
Access to information					
Access to informal network of alliances					
Perspective on organisation					
Access to decision-making processes					
Commitment from the powers that be					
Credibility of the individuals					
Influence of the individual					

Summary

Today, we looked briefly at the four bases of mentoring, and then went on to examine the organisational base in detail. This has two major dimensions: organisational readiness and positional strength. Tomorrow, we will go on to consider the second base: development.

The development base

Most situations in which mentoring takes place at work involve learning and development in one way or another. In fact, adapting to change is a key feature of modern working life. This means that we have constantly to adjust and develop. So learning becomes part of our way of life, for individuals as well as for organisations. In a learning organisation, learning and productive work are one and the same. It is therefore important that we pay some attention to how this takes place, and how we can encourage it.

In doing so, we will consider:

- Why learning is important
- How people learn at work
- The learning cycle
- Different styles of learning
- Learning to learn

Before we begin to examine why learning is so central to the business of mentoring, we should make an important distinction. Many people confuse the role of mentor with that of 'teacher' or 'tutor'. The roles are quite different. The focus of the roles of both teacher and tutor is the imparting of knowledge. Both roles are appropriate to the more school-based or academic education.

Mentoring is a much broader role than this, with a much wider focus. Although knowledge can be important, and coaching has a place in mentoring, it is not necessary that a mentor is an expert on all topics.

We shall explore these distinctions more thoroughly later on.

Why learning is important

In terms of learning at work, there are three factors that influence us and require that we learn and develop.

1 Work itself is changing   As markets, competitive forces and technology change, these put pressure on organisations to change. This in turn puts pressure on us to develop new ways of working. Change and development are wired in to most jobs, and these will involve us in continually learning new skills.

2 Career progression   Most of us have a need to progress within our jobs. For most of us this takes the form of the acquisition of responsibility and seniority. The days when we held the same job for life are gone.

As well as progression within a role or organisation, we often seek progression between jobs and organisations. Job mobility is now part of our way of professional life.

It is implicit in both of these factors that we develop and learn as we go along.

3 Personal satisfaction   Human beings have natural curiosity and need for variation. So we seek out opportunity, and this also involves a learning process.

However, in order for us to be able to learn, certain conditions need to be satisfied. These include:

- *Environmental conditions* such as resources, opportunity and support
- *Personal conditions* such as motivation, commitment and the ability to learn

In order to understand how we, as mentors can influence these, we need to look in more detail at how people go about learning at work.

Learning at work

For many of us, our attitudes to learning are framed by our experience of school and formal education. This version of learning usually involves a process that goes something like this:

a   There is a 'teacher' who is an expert, and knows everything

b   The 'teacher' tells us what we need to know, and/or how to do what we should be able to know/do

c   We then get it right and receive a pat on the head, or get it wrong and feel inadequate

This version of events has a number of important characteristics:

- It is highly dependent on the 'teacher', rather than the learner
- It concentrates on the acquisition of knowledge
- It is a hit-or-miss affair where 'failure' is regular and frowned upon

Of course, we don't want to suggest that all school, or even academic education takes the form of this description – just that it is many people's perception of learning.

The type of learning that we wish to concentrate on is different because adults are different to children, and because learning at work is different to formal or academic education.

We can summarise some of these differences:

Child learning
- Dependent on teacher
- Unrelated to experience
- Subject orientated
- Responsibility for learning rests with teacher

Adult learning
- Independent of tutor
- Relates to experience
- Responsibility rests with learner
- Work oriented
- Failure is tolerated

It should be clear from this that it is not appropriate for mentors to adopt the traditional role of a teacher. In the approach to adult learning implicit in the description above, the responsibility for the learning rests firmly with the learner. So what role then, does the mentor take? The answer is that a mentor can help learning in three basic ways. We shall call these:

- Facilitator
- Coach
- Learning consultant

The *facilitator* is someone who provides support and resources to the learner. One of the greatest resources, of course, is time. This might be the time that the mentor contributes, but also important is the time that the learner devotes to the process – not just in talking about things, but also in engaging in or trying out new activities, skills, and so on. The fact that mentors are usually more experienced and senior, and have greater influence within the organisation helps enormously in this aspect of the role.

The *coach* is one who is able to pass on skill or who is able to monitor and provide feedback to the learner as they attempt to develop skills or new behaviour. This will be dealt with more fully tomorrow.

The *learning consultant* is one who advises and helps the learner explicitly in the activity of learning. Encouragement and motivation are important here, because an adult learner might initially lack confidence in their own learning ability. It is why we have to accept or tolerate a level of failure. In fact, we shouldn't see it as failure, but as an unsuccessful trial from which we can learn.

In order for us to be successful as learning consultants, we should look in more detail at the process of learning as it applies to adults at work.

The learning cycle

A psychologist, David Kolb, has described learning as a circular process. This cycle of learning has four stages, which are necessary for learning to take place, as shown below.

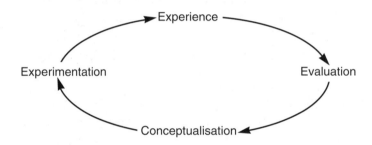

Experience
Work (and life) provide us with plenty of raw material for learning. This often comes in the form of things that go wrong. We all have the experience of sometimes ignoring these things, and therefore not learning from them.

Experience can also be more structured – such as that gained on training courses.

Evaluation
By the use of observation and reflection we can then begin to make sense of our experience. We can begin to notice what happens, and in what circumstances. At this stage we

may not yet know the rules of the game, but we are able to detect sequences of events that link together.

Conceptualisation

This is the analysis stage. It is where we frame answers to the question 'why does that happen?' We are able to construct theories and systems of explanations as to why the world behaves in the way it does.

Experimentation

In this phase we test or try out new behaviours based on the system of concepts we have built. Feedback will enable us to judge whether they are successful or not. Even if they are not, we still have some new experience, which returns us to another loop of the cycle.

This 'trial and error' description of learning is a natural process. It can tell us, as mentors, a number of things. First, by questioning behaviour, habits and assumptions, we can stimulate people to move through these phases of the learning process. Second, learning is a complex thing, and we need to give people the opportunity, or space to travel the journey in their own way. It helps to explain why just telling someone how to do something does not always work easily.

All learners will have different needs, strengths and weaknesses in relation to the phases of the learning cycle. These differences give rise to different approaches or styles of learning.

Learning styles

We can explain some of these differences by people's tendency to operate more often or comfortably in different phases of the cycle. Operating more strongly in one of the phases can be described as a particular style. So there are four basic styles of learning.

The *activist* learner is one who embraces immediate experience. They like the rush of adrenalin and will often take the lead in visible activities such as meetings and presentations.

Reflectors like to take their time and think carefully before acting. They tend to be cautious and measured in their approach.

Theorists are comfortable in the world of logic and ideas. They like to have a model or picture of a whole process or situation. They will find it difficult to do something if they do not know its purpose, or how it 'fits in'.

Pragmatists are the practical ones. They tend not to value theoretical knowledge too highly. When confronted with an idea or a plan they will ask 'but will it work?'

It is important to say that we all operate in all four phases of the cycle: nobody is only an activist, for instance. Most of us have a repertoire of behaviours that we can use in the appropriate circumstances. Equally, many of us have tendencies to learn consistently in one of these styles. Do you recognise yourself or people you know in these descriptions?

We should also point out that people can adjust and develop their style, by trying out new and unfamiliar behaviours.

But how does this help us as mentors? If we recognise that someone fits strongly into one of these styles, what do we do? One option is to respect that and tailor learning activities that will suit that style. The other option is to encourage them to do something unfamiliar, or even uncomfortable.

The best response is to do both. In the early stages we will gain rapport and trust by recognising and respecting people's preferred way of learning. However, once the learner has built confidence in themselves as a learner, one of the great contributions we can make is to help them to try something new.

One of the great satisfactions of mentoring is to see the highly reflective 'shrinking violet' come out of their shell and confidently give a presentation. We can encourage the activist who wades in at the deep end (and often drowns) to step back and think before acting, and to make judgements about the practicality and viability of their options.

You can read more about the concept of learning styles in the *Manual of Learning Styles* (1992) P. Honey and N. Mumford, Maidenhead.

Learning to learn

Some people are more efficient and experienced at learning. For many adults at work, it may have been a long time since they have engaged actively in learning. Such 'naïve' learners may lack confidence in the early stages of a programme, and may need patience and support until they gain more confidence.

'Mature' learners, on the other hand, will have confidence and will be more self-sufficient in relation to their learning.

How can a mentor make a judgement about how 'mature' their learner is? Experience tells us that there are a number of key indicators:

- The capacity to set high but achievable goals
- The level of responsibility they take for their own learning
- Previous experience in the subject to be learned
- Previous educational experience

On the basis of these factors, we should be able to make a judgement about a learner's ability to learn. It is worth doing this because this level of learner maturity does influence the way that we mentor them.

The main difference in the way we would mentor learners at different ends of the scale is found in the level of direction.

Naïve learners may need a higher level of direction – particularly early on in a programme. They are likely to perceive a higher level of direction as being quite appropriate. Of course, it should also be a part of your agenda to help them to increase their level of learning efficiency. This can be done by paying attention to the first two of the factors in the list above. In these circumstances, success breeds success.

Mature and efficient learners will need less direction. By definition, they are used to setting high but achievable goals. They are more likely to perceive a high level of direction as inappropriate or as interfering.

By using the ideas in this section, we can tailor our mentoring style more closely to the needs of our learner. These will affect the nature of that relationship, so we shall now look in more detail at the relationship base of mentoring.

Summary

The development base covers everything to do with learning. Everyone has a different style of learning and as a mentor, we need to realise this and adjust our 'mentoring style' accordingly. Learners may even have to 'learn how to learn', which is something we have to be aware of. We also looked at the learning cycle which sums up exactly how we learn.

Tomorrow, we will look at the interpersonal base.

The interpersonal or relationship base

The nature and quality of the individual relationship between the mentor and the learner is of course the key to success. In setting out ideas about the conduct of this relationship we shall consider these factors:

- Core conditions
- Counselling
- Coaching
- Levels of intervention

Core conditions

There are certain factors, or core conditions that are necessary for such a relationship at work to be successful.

Mentoring relationships, particularly where they arise naturally, go beyond normal professional working relationships. They engage both the mentor and the learner in a deeper and more personal way, and their focus is not merely on the task in hand.

Research has shown that positive and beneficial relationships such as these tend to satisfy certain conditions, and these imply a certain orientation from the mentor.

There are three core conditions:

- Rapport
- Positive regard
- Congruence

Rapport is the state achieved when some person (like a mentor) is able to 'lock in' to the information being provided by the other person. It involves noticing and recognising verbal and non-verbal information. At the conscious level it also involves being able to understand and appreciate the other person's point of view.

This state is perfectly natural for us, and occurs in all of our most intimate relationships.

Positive regard is being able to accept without judgement or interpretation, the other person, their point of view, opinions, personality, and so on. It is being able to take them 'for what they are'.

Congruence is characterised by openness, spontaneity and genuineness. It occurs when there is a consistency between our words and our behaviour.

Added to these more general concepts are specific
behaviours or skills that are necessary for the maintenance
of the relationship.

Maintenance tasks/features
- Accessibility
- Giving feedback
- Appropriate questioning technique
- Communication skills
- Knowledge of learner

Two of these deserve some attention in detail.

Giving feedback
We need to be constructive and positive as well as honest in
the way that we give feedback. The feedback cycle is crucial
to the development of the individual. For some people it is
easy to be harsh or overcritical – in other words to play the
expert. For others it is easy to be nice without ever giving
positive criticism. It is this positive criticism that can often
be the most helpful.

When giving feedback, you should bear in mind the
following:

Feedback should focus on:
- Behaviour not the person
- Observations rather than inferences or guesses
- Description rather than judgement
- The specific rather than the general
- Factors under the control of the learner

Knowledge of the individual

It is worthwhile remembering that at the outset, or during the course of any relationship, there are a great many pieces of information that we learn, or are offered, about an individual that will inform the relationship. Among these are:

- Motivation
- Experience
- Personal goals
- Approach or personality
- Learning style and maturity

It obviously makes sense to adjust our approach to the individual to take account of these factors. They do not entail a set of rules, nor are they prescriptive, but they should make us sensitive to the needs and style of operation of our learners.

It is difficult to summarise or provide a single message from our consideration of the core conditions that surround a mentor–learner relationship. However, running through them all is a theme of empowering people. That is, the object is to help people to make their own decisions and to learn in a way that is comfortable for them, whilst providing resources which enable them to use the opportunities available to them to their maximum benefit.

Counselling and coaching

The two key roles which a mentor can adopt are those of counsellor and coach. Traditionally, the coach is seen as someone who assists in the development of a skill or technique, whilst the counsellor is seen as a solver of personal problems.

We would like to question this dichotomy. Coaching and counselling exist at either ends of a continuum which has the process or task at one end, and the individual at the other. At both ends of this continuum there can be problems, and both are framed by skill and goals.

At either end of the scale, the focus might be different, and the skills of the mentor must shift according to the priorities. We will set out here an approach to both of these roles, but we must emphasise that the repertoire of skills and qualities required for both have a large amount of overlap.

Counselling

The more person-centred type of intervention requires a knowledge of the basic counselling process.

Counselling can be thought of as a three-stage process:

1 Information/understanding
2 Solutions
3 Action

Information/understanding
This is where rapport is established between the two people. The aim will be for the learner to arrive at a cogent definition of the problem, and for the mentor to arrive at an understanding of it.

The key skill here is that of active listening. That is, listening which gives the agenda to the talker. Questions should be open, i.e. should not entail a yes/no answer. Understanding should be checked. Interpretation should be minimised.

Solutions
At this stage there are two broad aims. The first one is for the learner to achieve a redefinition of the problem. The process of going through phase one often leads people to a new view of a situation, or new insights. At this stage they are ready to invent options and to define outcomes, or to set goals. We have already said that both creativity and flexibility are important at this stage. Creativity is required in helping to develop options, and flexibility in respecting options that work for the learner, whatever the preference of the mentor.

Up until now, the mentor may have intervened verbally very little – the key contribution being allowing and encouraging the learner to talk. But at this stage, the style of questioning shifts a little. It can become more challenging and probing. The use of 'Why', 'What would happen if . . .', 'Are you sure . . .' type of questions becomes appropriate.

Action
This phase is really about making plans, implementing and managing solutions that arise from goals set at the previous phase. The skill is in allowing people to develop realistic and appropriate strategies, and in providing resources for those strategies.

The formal and systematic approach to counselling set out above has been established through experience and practice over many years. However, it is worth pointing out that like many interpersonal skills, it is a perfectly natural process practised by good counsellors – whether they think they know about it or not!

Perhaps you have had the experience of a friend phoning you up with a problem of a personal nature. It is a quite common experience that however little you talk (or think you contribute) that they will thank you for clearing up a problem for them. If you think about such an experience in retrospect you might realise how the conversation fell naturally into the phases outlined above.

Coaching

As we have said, coaching is aimed at the development of skills or techniques, and can be thought of as a specific kind of counselling intervention. What sets it apart from the more general type of counselling is that the goals or outcomes are already known, and they are usually behaviourally specific. It is therefore very useful in the development of competence.

The model set out here is adapted from *Coaching for Performance* by John Whitmore, who sees coaching as involving four phases:

1 Set **G**oals for overall application and individual session
2 Setting out the current position, or **R**eality
3 Generating **O**ptions with plans and strategies
4 Decide **W**hat is to be done, by whom, when and how

Progress through the **GROW** model is enhanced by questioning and feedback, rather than by instruction.

Goals
Goals set should be **SMART**. That is, they should be:

Specific
Measurable
Achievable
Realistic
Time related

We all have goals like, 'I want to be happy', but if they do not correspond to the criteria above, we will be unlikely to achieve them. The two key features of goals in this context are that we should have a way (or test) to confirm when we have achieved them, and they should be set by the learner themselves.

However, we mentioned in the section on learning that a low maturity learner may need considerable help to define goals, particularly if they relate to an area of operations with which they are unfamiliar.

Reality
This stage is really an ecology check. It concerns all of the facts, figures, resources and people surrounding the goals at stage one.

Let us give an example. Suppose a learner has decided that to improve their interviewing skills, they will conduct an upcoming interview for a member of staff in their department. This may satisfy all of the **SMART** criteria for a goal. However, the organisation might have procedures and practices to follow. The personnel department may expect to conduct the interview. Colleagues may have a vested interest. All of the surrounding factors need to be taken into account when deciding upon a course of action.

Options

This corresponds quite closely with phase two of the counselling model. As with counselling, both the generation and selection of options needs a substantial amount of creativity and flexibility from the mentor.

Sometimes, the appropriate option may be obvious to the mentor but not the learner. At what stage, or level to intervene is a complex issue, and is discussed below.

What

It is here that specific plans and courses of action are defined. The allocation of responsibilities and resources are agreed by mentor and learner. Again, monitoring and feedback are essential to the successful completion of this stage.

You may have noticed that not only is there a great deal of correspondence between the processes of counselling and coaching, but that there is also synergy between the coaching process and Kolb's model of learning (see Wednesday).

Both counselling and coaching encourage learners to reflect on their experience, identifying and conceptualising the key issues, in order to develop plans of action with which to test (experiment) against experience.

Levels of intervention

Throughout this text we have emphasised the importance of empowering the learner to make their own decisions, set their own goals, and of assisting them to solve their own problems.

We can help to make sense of this by looking at the ways, or more accurately the levels, at which it is possible for a mentor to intervene in the learning process.

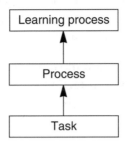

Task

If a learner has a very specific problem it is possible (and sometimes very tempting) to intervene and solve that problem for them. In acute circumstances it is sometimes necessary to do so.

In such situations we are acting as a consultant or expert, and providing a solution. What we offer in such cases is our specialist knowledge.

Process

Another approach would be to enable the learner to learn or develop the correct solution-finding procedure. In other words we can teach them the process by which they can solve many similar problems or classes of problems. We would then be a process consultant.

What we offer here is the development of skill, and this is more useful than solutions to a specific task because it is more general and more widely applicable.

Learning to learn

At this level, we are a learning-process manager, or learning facilitator. Here we encourage people to teach themselves how to find solutions. This is the most general level at which we can intervene. It is therefore the most useful and the most powerful. Not surprisingly, it is also the most difficult.

It is also worth saying that most learners need to gain confidence and 'find their feet' at the lower levels, before they are ready for the abstractness and ambiguity of the higher levels.

However, as learners gain that confidence, they become ready for the challenge of learning to learn for themselves. This can be considered the end point of a successful and mature relationship. If your mentoring relationship graduates to this level, you have, by definition mastered all of the ideas set out in this book.

Summary

The interpersonal base is all about building a relationship between mentor and learner, and then managing it. We saw how feedback is incredibly important, but we need to be careful that we give the right sort of feedback: to be overcritical can be damaging.

As a mentor we adopt a role. We saw that we can be either counsellors or coaches, with each of these roles involving slightly different methods of dealing with people.

Tomorrow we go on to look at the final mentoring base: context.

The context base

The context base of mentoring is all about the specific details of the scheme or individual relationship. Each scheme, programme or relationship will be quite different in the demands it makes on a mentor (and a learner). However, it is possible to outline several broad considerations that you as a mentor need to consider if your relationship is to be successful. We can view the important elements of the context base in four categories:

- Types of programme
- Objectives
- Who mentors whom
- Terms of reference

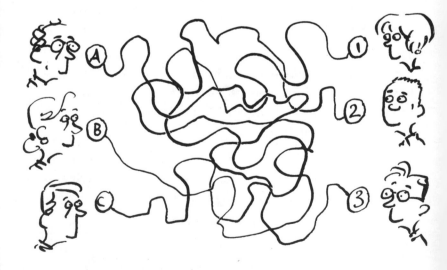

Types of programme

We mentioned on Sunday some of the different types of situation in which mentoring can take place. These included:

- Induction of staff
- Career progression or development
- Learning programmes

Each of these can differ in the level of formality and the level of their systematisation. So within these specific applications there are a number of factors or issues that are worth consideration.

Open-frame mentoring
This style tends to the less formal, with very few specific objectives or deliverables. Usually, the mentor is called upon on the basis of need. It tends to be non-directive mentoring.

Project-based mentoring
This is where there is a specifically defined work-based deliverable or outcome. The mentor will help to define, plan, implement and complete the project in question, and to help the learner to identify and satisfy learning requirements on the way. Some networks of peers operate mutual mentoring on such a project basis.

Qualification-based programmes
More usually found in management development contexts.
The programmes may range from in-company provision
through to NVQ management programmes or MBAs. They
usually involve quite specific learning objectives, rather than
business objectives, and a high level of self-assessment. The
support offered on non-management programmes tends to
be more like that of a tutor than the more complete role of
mentor that we have outlined in this book.

You might like to think how each of these types of approach
can affect the mentoring relationship. How do the
requirements differ? It might be worthwhile thinking about
programmes of which you have experience (or are about to
experience), and how they fit into the descriptions given.

Objectives

Any differences of approach will be reflected in the
objectives related to the programme. These objectives will
operate at two levels.

Objectives carried into the programme
These will be the organisational priorities for the
programme in question, and have been discussed in that
section. However, it is important that these are visible,
shared and agreed upon by both mentor and learner. Where
these objectives are quite general, it is part of the role of the
mentor to help the learner to translate these into specific and
personally relevant objectives, and if necessary, renegotiate
where appropriate.

Personal objectives of the learner

These may take the form of statements of outcomes from the programme, or they may be specific learning objectives that arise *en route*. In general, the objectives of both learner and organisation should be compatible. It is important early on in the relationship that a mentor checks out that this is the case, and monitors the situation for any source of potential conflict. Agreement and communication, are, of course, essential at this stage.

The objectives of the programme should also help you as a mentor, to decide what you need to know, and what the learner needs to know. But as well as the objectives, the processes for managing the scheme should be in place at this stage, along with the resources to implement it. One important resource may be the training of the mentors. On structured programmes this should involve at least a briefing about the details of the programme. It may also involve training of the skills related to the role.

Processes for managing a scheme should include monitoring and evaluative components. How are mentors going to give feedback to the scheme? How will they communicate with each other?

All of this information will help you to clarify your role and responsibilities, and to define the limits of your intervention.

Case-study

The Institute of Management has recently introduced a mentoring scheme to support the career development of its employees and has identified the following objectives:

1 To provide a source of skill and career guidance and support available to all staff
2 To help staff in the development and implementation of their own career development plans
3 To supplement and support activities of managers in developing their staff

The scheme is entirely voluntary, both for mentors and learners. It is not part of the management process of the Institute or its performance appraisal scheme.

Who mentors who?

Informal and unstructured mentoring relationships develop on the basis of mutual interest and satisfaction. In more, organised schemes or programmes there may be more selection or conscription. Obviously, volunteers and mutual choice are the ideal, but this may not always be possible or practical. Assigned mentor relationships can work very well, although good programmes allow both mentors and learners the right of veto. As a mentor, an important point to check early on is whether your learner is a volunteer or a conscript, as this will affect the relationship.

Of course, there are also many varieties of relationships between these two extremes. An example would be where a pool of mentors is selected and trained, and learners can then select their own mentor from the pool. This increases the likelihood of the relationship working. This is very close to the way the Institute of Management scheme, above works.

One often discussed question is whether a line manager should be a mentor. We believe that mentoring should be a component of any line manager–subordinate relationship.

However, for more organised or formal schemes, this is not always the ideal arrangement. Mentor–learner relationships should proceed in an atmosphere of openness and trust. They need to be bounded by confidentiality. They need to be unrelated to issues of promotion, appraisal or salary. It is possible for the mentor relationship and the line manager relationship to suffer from a conflict of interest. It is therefore best to avoid this if there is an alternative option. Remember, choosing the alternative option does not reflect on the integrity of any particular line manager. Rather the learner has much more to gain by widening his or her perspective through knowledge and experience provided by another objective individual outside the line.

As mentioned above, training is important – particularly in organised programmes. You should try to define your own needs in respect of this training, in order both to maximise on the training, and to pay attention to your own development throughout the programme.

Terms of reference

Role responsibilities and expectations have already been mentioned. You should be able to articulate these expectations and boundaries, and discuss them with your learner. In this way, there will be no mismatch of expectations which are a common cause of the failure of many mentor–learner relationships.

These expectations should be drawn up into terms of reference. If they are not provided by the organisation, it can be a useful starting point in developing the way in which you are going to work, to draw them up together. They also help to ensure that there is a consistency of purpose and responsibility between you.

They should include the following:

Confidentiality Who gets to hear what? Should mentors discuss issues that arise with other people? What are the restrictions?

Communication How do mentors communicate with learners, with each other, with the organisation?

Timetable What guidelines are available? How often should mentor and learner meet? Is there a defined end point?

Support If the relationship is not working, what happens? Who mentors and supports mentors?

Responsibilities Are the responsibilities defined for mentor, learner, line manager, scheme sponsor?

The following examples show how the differing circumstances in which mentoring takes place result in specific terms of reference.

Case-studies

NHS Wales A management development officer visits mentors once every three to four months to assess learners progress and monitor the relationships.

A large chemical company Sets out that mentors should:

- Meet the learner once a month, for an hour, by timetabling formally in advance
- Ensure the learner maintains a brief diary of daily events, to form the basis for monthly discussions
- Develop a personal relationship with the learner
- Maintain the relationship for two years

British Gas South East This mentoring scheme was introduced to help graduates who must make frequent job moves within the company during their first few years of development. The aim is to produce a four-way link between mentor, learner, line manager and training department. A key role for the training department is communication. They have published guidelines for the conduct of the relationship, detailing, for example, the time commitment graduates need to give to the programme, and specific development projects and frequency of meetings (at least once every two months).

AMI Healthcare   These have introduced a mentoring
scheme specifically for senior managers on the
company's executive development programme.
Mentors have a requirement to support project work
which covers an area of work unfamiliar to the learner.
Mentors are also expected to have a role in the
informal assessment of learners.

These examples may serve to give you some idea of the
variety of modes of operation of mentoring programmes.

We are now ready for the final stage – the implementation
of the mentoring programme.

Summary

In order to be able to mentor effectively, the context has to
be established. This means deciding what type of
programme to follow and what its objectives are. It also
involves deciding who mentors whom and what the terms
of references are for the mentoring relationship. This
involves establishing just what is expected from both learner
and mentor during the developmental process.

The chapter also included overviews of several case-studies
to show how mentoring works in 'real life'.

Tomorrow, we conclude by looking at implementing
mentoring schemes.

Implementing mentoring schemes

Now that we have covered every aspect of the role of mentoring, we need to pay attention to the practicalities of implementing schemes. In doing so, we will consider:

- Factors affecting a scheme
- Designing a scheme
- Implementing a scheme
- Mentoring checklist
- Sources of further information

In terms of scale, there are of course differences between formal and informal schemes. In general, the guidance that follows may seem to be more relevant to formal schemes. However, the issues discussed apply to informal situations just as much, even though the need for planning and the organisation and commitment of resources is less.

Throughout the book we have based our ideas on the four-base model of mentoring. A potential mentor who has read through and noted the guidance here should now be equipped for the role. What we shall present here is a summary of the key considerations, set out in the order in which the implementation of the process takes place.

Factors affecting a scheme

The first consideration with a major scheme which has a mentoring component is the organisation in which the development activity will take place. If it provides the right environment and resources, much of the rest can follow naturally. Introducing a scheme is a major project, and should be treated as such. The key areas of activity can now be considered:

- A supportive work culture/environment
- Participants are volunteers
- Selection is discriminating
- Defined objectives and time frame
- Training and development in content/structure/ purposes of scheme and personal skills
- Terms of reference
- Monitoring

These factors all help to make a successful scheme. In planning a scheme, consideration should be given to which ones are in place, how to put others in place, and how you can manage without any of the factors.

There is one other key factor that we have found by experience to be critical. Schemes or major development programmes need a champion. In our research and experience with many in-company management programmes, the successful ones invariably had a champion role model.

Although we have stressed the need for top management commitment, and that the support of a senior figurehead can add weight, importance and impetus to a programme, this is not what we necessarily think of as a champion. The role of the champion needs more than words, or even visibility. It can be fulfilled in a number of ways.

The first way it can be achieved is by role modelling and 'walking the talk'. In other words we will have a situation where a senior manager or director does some or all of the following:

The role model champion
- Shows visible support and commitment
- Shows commitment to the priorities and results of the scheme
- Plays a part in the development of the programme
- Will be trained with colleagues and subordinates
- Gets to know the people involved in the scheme
- Becomes a contributing mentor

Another version of the champion role is the person (often less senior than the role model champion) who runs the programme or manages the project. They will do many of the following:

Project manager champion
- Takes overall responsibility for the scheme
- Coordinates all of the activities
- Provides the focus of communication
- Becomes the source of information/advice
- Becomes the mentor's mentor
- Provides the contact with external bodies/suppliers

The contribution that the project manager champion makes is to 'oil the wheels' and keep all involved on track. In our experience, very often, the success of a scheme can be attributed directly to the project manager champion.

Developing a scheme

A development scheme is an activity or project much like any other work based initiative. So it needs the application of the planning cycle, and managing, like any such project.

The planning or managing cycle sets out the steps in carrying out a major task in logical time order.

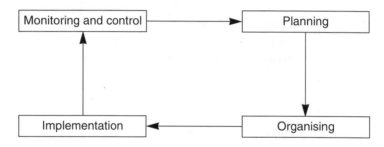

At the planning stage, these are the major considerations:

- Objectives
- Structure
- Resources
- Selection
- Training
- Plans and time frames

The detailed consideration of each of these can be found in the appropriate section of the text. There is, however, one resource that is often ignored or underestimated, and that is time. It is important to pay attention to the time needed by both mentors and learners in any structured scheme.

- When will the mentoring take place?
- Will meetings/sessions be scheduled or programmed?
- Will it be considered as a legitimate activity in its own right?
- Can 'quality' time be freed up for the required purposes?

It is surprising how often major schemes are planned on the tacit assumption that mentoring is an extra activity, and will somehow just happen on its own. It often does not.

Implementation

It is always anticipated that projects will roll out according to plan. In a perfect world they always would. Unfortunately, things do not always work in a perfect way. Much of the skill of delivering or implementing a successful programme comes from adjusting according to events, and in particular, according to needs as they arise. The following ideas might help:

- Communication
- Support
- Performance goals and indicators
- Monitoring and ongoing evaluation

Communication
Good lines and mechanisms for communication should be incorporated into any good plans. However, some of the needs will only become apparent in the run time. A good

project manager, and a good plan, will make provision for emerging needs. These needs might take different forms. They might include the need for:

- Feedback to be shared
- Problems to be shared and dealt with
- Mentor or learner to network

Support

The need for good support mechanisms has been emphasised throughout. If adequate processes and resources are put into place, then problems can be dealt with without threatening the success of the programme.

Performance goals and indicators

Of course, goals and objectives are important. But global goals need to be translated to the level of the individual learner and the individual mentor. The learner should have clear goals. But how do you, as mentor, know if your intervention is effective or successful? These goals can be framed in terms of performance, in terms of stages reached, in terms of skill or capability, in terms of attitude, or in terms of the relationship.

Indicators or 'signposts' are a way of defining steps along the route to success. It is important for both mentor and learner to put in some measures prior to the culmination of the process that let you know that things are going well.

Monitoring and evaluation

Having defined indicators, we now have a way of knowing whether we are achieving our goals. This is important in terms of the motivation and satisfaction of the individuals, as well as the success of the whole scheme. Again, processes need to be in place to evaluate properly, and to adjust according to experience. This will need to involve sharing information outside the particular relationship. What provisions are made for this?

Agenda for first meeting

The first meeting is where the style and tone of the relationship is set. From the learner's point of view, it can often involve uncertainty and anxiety. It is important as a mentor to prepare yourself for the first meeting.

So what should happen at a first meeting? Here are some of the issues you might need to discuss:

- Life histories/experience
- Job roles and responsibilities
- Purposes/goals of scheme
- Terms of reference/confidentiality
- Signposts and targets
- Nature of relationship
- Times, when and where, how often
- Assessment of individual – skills, needs, personal goals etc.
- Future meetings

It is impossible to be prescriptive, but within all of these topics there are two things that carry special importance.

The major priority in the first and early meetings is to establish the relationship itself. Gaining rapport, trust and confidence are building platforms for productive and satisfying activity. This is a skill in its own right, and you need to pay conscious attention to it.

The other element of first, and early meetings is meeting discipline. Some relationships will be naturally low key and open frame. But where there are detailed and specific purposes, and work to do, then there is a message or role model responsibility to lead by example. You should therefore come prepared, agree agendas and keep to time. This is a good skill and discipline that you can pass on to the learner.

Problems

Within even the best planned scheme, it is possible, and even likely that problems may occur. Good planning, however, should enable you to prevent major, structural problems. The major ones to avoid are:

- *Political problems* – where vested interests conflict with the aims of the scheme
- *Extra tasks/responsibilities* – where new or arbitrary requirements disrupt the running
- *Relationship* – such as wrong mentor, lack of rapport, mentor leaving

What should be anticipated and dealt with are the minor run-time difficulties that an individual learner might experience on any learning programme. Some of these might be learning difficulties which can be dealt with by good communication skills and good coaching. Others might be practical difficulties, which may need the experience and expertise of the mentor to solve directly, or to assist the learner to solve.

Some examples to be prepared for are:

Practical problems
- Learner too busy
- Poor time management
- Obstructive line manager
- Lack of opportunity/access/information
- Competence need – 'I don't know how to . . .'
- Mentor need – 'I don't know either . . .'

Winding up a scheme

Most mentoring projects or schemes will have a natural life cycle. This will progress from, possibly, tentative beginnings, through maturity, to end. It should be planned and agreed at the beginning both how and when the relationship will end. It is not good for anyone for important relationships just to cease. The way to avoid this is to discuss and agree a natural endpoint. A proper wind-down and exit should happen, so that both parties can properly readjust to life without the relationship.

Mentoring checklist

Finally, we set out here a comprehensive checklist that will help in the planning and implementing of mentor schemes – whatever their scope or nature. The points on the checklist can serve as prompts, either to direct you back into the text, or for further thought or planning.

- Right organisation?
- Identified right mentors?
- Scheme evaluation in place?
- Top management commitment?
- Resources?
- Selection and training?
- Matching mentors to learners?
- Terms of reference/guidelines for scheme?
- Contingency plans to deal with problems?
- Support for mentors?

Further sources of information

If you wish to read or find out more about mentoring, the Institute of Management can provide the following:

- *The Essential Guide to Mentoring* (with supplements for mentoring in NVQ management programmes)
- Comprehensive booklist and literature search (available from the Management Information Centre)
- Personal/individual counselling or mentoring
- Consultancy on in-company mentoring schemes

For details of any of these, please contact:

Steve Carter, Institute of Management, 0536 204222.

The Successful Business in a Week series

Successful Appraisals in a Week
Successful Assertiveness in a Week
Successful Budgeting in a Week
Successful Business Writing in a Week
Successful Career Planning in a Week
Finance for Non-Financial Managers in a Week
Successful Interviewing in a Week
Understanding Just in Time in a Week
Successful Leadership in a Week
Successful Marketing in a Week
Successful Market Research in a Week
Successful Meetings in a Week
Successful Motivation in a Week
Successful Presentation in a Week
Successful Project Management in a Week
Successful Public Relations in a Week
Successful Negotiating in a Week
Successful Selling in a Week
Successful Stress Management in a Week
Successful Time Management in a Week
Understanding Total Quality Management in a Week
Doing Business in Europe